Delays in Court Cases in India
By Siva Prasad Bose and Joy Bose

Published by Joy Bose

Copyright © 2021, 2025 Siva Prasad Bose

All rights reserved
No part of this book may be reproduced, or stored in a retrieval system, or transmitted in any form or by any means, electronic, mechanical, photocopying, recording, or otherwise, without express written permission of the publisher.

Contents

Dedication

Preface

1. Problem of delays in court cases

2. Delays in court cases related to property disputes

3. Delays in criminal cases

4. Delays in court cases related to family disputes

5. Problem of lack of judges

6. Delays by police and government agencies

7. Intentional delays by litigants

8. Public Interest Litigation (PILs)

9. Recommendations to speed up court cases

10. Judicial Reforms in India

11. Conclusion

About the Author

Glossary of Key Terms

Other Books by Siva Prasad Bose

Dedication

This book is dedicated to all those litigants who are suffering from long delays in their court cases filed in Indian courts.

Preface

The Indian court system today carries one of the heaviest burdens in the world. Cases move slowly, hearings are short, and backlogs run into crores. For many litigants, a court case does not feel like a path to justice but a long period of uncertainty, expense and stress. When disputes remain unresolved for years, sometimes decades, ordinary citizens lose faith in the very system meant to protect their rights.

This book aims to explain, in plain language, why delays occur and what can be done to fix them. We look at how different kinds of cases, such as property disputes, criminal matters, family conflicts, get stuck at various stages. We examine the role of police and government agencies, the shortage of judges, outdated procedures, and even the tactics used by litigants to prolong cases. We also discuss how technology, including recent advances such as AI tools and digital courts, is beginning to reshape the justice system.

The goal of this book is simple: to help readers understand the scale of the problem and the reforms needed to make justice faster, fairer and more accessible. Improving the system will require both political will and administrative effort, but the solutions are within reach if pursued with seriousness and consistency.

Chapter 1: Problem of delays in court cases

The Indian court system has the problem of slow disposal of justice, with some court cases taking decades to get a verdict. In this chapter, we discuss the scale of the problem by sharing some data about the number of pending cases and how long it takes to resolve them.

As the saying goes, justice delayed is justice denied. Cases pending for a long time lead to unnecessary stress and financial costs for litigants, and may result in denial of justice altogether. In criminal cases, this leads to undertrials languishing in prison for years despite their guilt not being proved. Therefore, this delay of resolution is a problem that urgently needs tackling.

1.1 Time taken for disposal of court cases

The civil cases in Indian courts typically take years or decades to resolve, from the time when the case is started till the time the final verdict is made by the court. In this section we discuss the average time taken in various cases.

An article in the Wire magazine analyzed government data to find that 37 lakhs cases took 0–20 years to reach a verdict, 6.4 lakh cases took 20–30 years and about 2 lakh cases took more than 30 years.

The recent Covid-19 pandemic and the subsequent lockdown has worsened the situation. As per a report by India today, between Jan to Sep 2020, the number of cases increased by 12.4% in high courts and 6.6% in lower courts.

Figure: Graph showing the number of cases, with time taken to resolve them (in years)

One important reason for the long time taken for disposal of cases is the high number of pending court cases, as we see in the following section.

1.2 High number of pending court cases

India has almost 4 crore total pending cases in Supreme court, high courts and lower courts, as of 2020. This is as per a written reply by the government in parliament, published in a Bloomberg quint article. Of these 70% are civil cases and remaining 30% are criminal cases. In the high courts and supreme courts, most of the pending cases are civil cases, while the criminal cases are more in lower courts. This number has further increased since then because of the Covid-19 lockdowns, and is close to 4.5 crore.

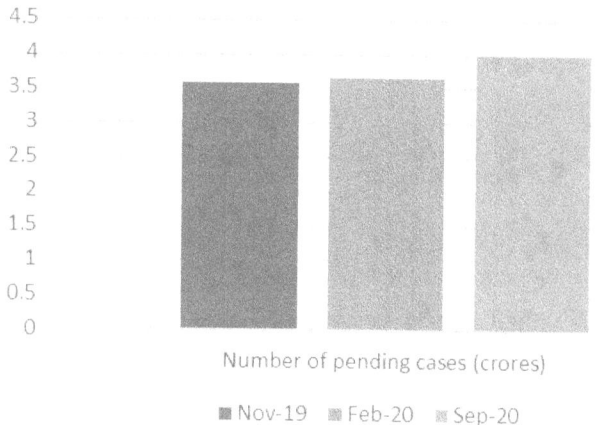

Figure: Graph showing growth in numbers of total pending cases in various Indian courts.

Among these, Allahabad high court had the highest number of cases, followed by Punjab and Haryana High Court and Madras High Court, while the high courts in north eastern states had relatively lower numbers of pending cases.

There are around 10000 courts in India, including one supreme court, 25 high courts and the remaining lower courts including district courts. The approximate breakdown of the number of cases in various courts is as follows, as per the cited data from National Judicial Data grid.

- Supreme Court — 69000 pending cases
- High courts — 58.5 lakh cases
- Lower courts — 3.9 crore pending cases

Here too, in high courts almost a quarter of the cases were pending for over 10 years.

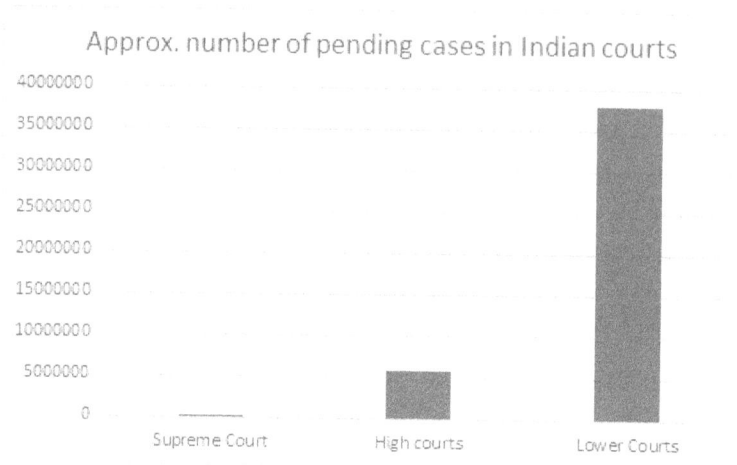

Figure: Graph showing approximate number of pending cases in different types of courts

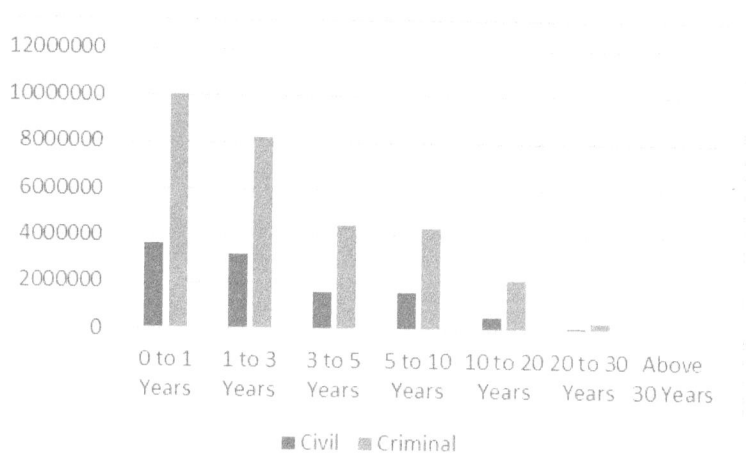

Figure: Graph showing number and time taken for civil and criminal cases pending in lower courts (District and Taluka courts), as per the data from the National Judicial Data Grid

1.3 High number of undertrials in prison in criminal court cases

Due to pending criminal cases, the number of undertrials in prison was more than double (70%) of the number of convicts, as per a 2020 report in the Hindu newspaper. 3.28 lakh prison inmates were undergoing trial in 2020. 1.6 crore criminal cases were pending for more than a year, while 22 lakh cases were pending for more than 10 years. Due to this, the period of confinement increased for undertrials.

This is especially worrying because the undertrials are those whose guilt is not proven and have not yet been convicted by the court, but they are still in jail rather than out on bail. The principles of "innocent until proven guilty" and the right to liberty enshrined in the Indian constitution seem to be getting violated due to this.

1.4 Multiple dates and less time for hearings

The phrase "Tareekh pe Tareekh" by Sunny Deol from the famous Bollywood movie, Damini, is a reality in Indian courts today. Cases typically keep getting next date after next date, without receiving enough time for a proper hearing in the court.

As per a recent report by India today based on a survey by Daksh, the average time for each hearing in Patna high court was just 2 minutes.

1.5 Slow disposal rate in the courts

As per a report by PRS legislative research, the disposal rate for court cases is between 28% to 55% in various courts in India. This means that fewer number of cases get disposed each year compared to the number of fresh cases filed. Because of this, the number of cases keep increasing year by year.

1.6 Public Perception and Loss of Faith

Citizens increasingly view courts as inaccessible, slow, and unaffordable. This perception gap between constitutional ideals and ground reality has led many to avoid formal courts altogether, opting for informal or extrajudicial mechanisms instead.

1.7 Conclusion

In this chapter we have gone through a few statistics of the slow disposal of cases and high number of pending cases in the Indian courts. The scale of the problem is huge and hence, a solution is urgently needed.

References:

1. Madan B Lokur, The Wire. What Is Stopping Our Justice System From Tackling the Cases Pending Before Courts? 12 May 2021. Available: https://thewire.in/law/india-judiciary-pending-cases-supreme-court

2. Pradip Kumar Das, Legal Service India. Justice Delayed is Justice Denied. Available: https://www.legalserviceindia.com/article/l317-Justice-Delayed-is-Justice-Denied.html

3. PRS Legislative Research. Pendency of cases in the judiciary. Available: https://prsindia.org/policy/vital-stats/pendency-cases-judiciary

4. Kaushik Deka, India Today. On India's Judiciary: Bogged By A Backlog. Jan 30 2021. Available: https://www.indiatoday.in/magazine/nation/story/20210208-bogged-by-a-backlog-1763840-2021-01-30

5. Harish Narsappa, India Today. The long, expensive road to justice. April 2016. Available: https://www.indiatoday.in/magazine/cover-story/story/20160509-judicial-system-judiciary-cji-law-cases-the-long-expensive-road-to-justice-828810-2016-04-27

6. Bloomberg Quint. India's pending court cases on the rise: In charts. 29 September 2020. Available: https://www.bloombergquint.com/law-and-policy/indias-pending-court-cases-on-the-rise-in-charts

7. Vignesh Radhakrishnan and Sumant Sen, the Hindu. 70% prisoners in India are undertrials. Sep 2020. Available: https://www.thehindu.com/data/data-70-prisoners-in-india-are-undertrials/article32569643.ece

8. National Judicial Data Grid. Available: https://njdg.ecourts.gov.in/njdgnew/index.php

9. Kenneth Mohanty, News18. Explained: CJI Ramana Says 4.5 Crore Cases Pending, Here's What Has Been Fuelling Backlog In Indian Courts. July 2021. Available: https://www.news18.com/news/explainers/explained-cji-ramana-says-4-5-crore-cases-pending-heres-what-has-been-fuelling-backlog-3977411.html

Chapter 2: Delays in court cases related to property disputes

Pending property cases are the longest pending and the highest number (about 66%) clogging the Indian court system. Therefore, in this chapter we focus on such cases and discuss some of the reasons for the pendency of property disputes in Indian courts, along with related data where available.

Property and land disputes are bad for all parties involved. They lead to high litigation costs with no productive results, and are a burden on the economy. Sometimes the property disputes take decades or even generations to resolve. Often, they are related to inheritance and succession within the same family, in which case they further lead to bad blood within the family. Such disputes affect all classes of people: even the richest families of industrialists are not immune to them.

Therefore, it is essential to have procedures to clear the current backlog of such cases and some clear guidelines for speedy resolution in the future.

2.1 Data on the scale of property disputes in India

A 2016 newspaper article, based on a study by Daksh, mentioned that land and property cases account for two thirds of all pending civil court cases in India, including 7.5 million civil cases. Total cost of such litigation was 0.5% of India's GDP.

Another report by Center for policy research (CPR) found the following:

- Property disputes affect around 7.7 million people in India.

- Property disputes clog every level of courts in India from district and lower courts to supreme court.

- Property disputes are the largest both in terms of absolute numbers and time taken to resolve the cases.

- About 25% of all cases decided by the Supreme Court involve property disputes.

- Property disputes make up 66% of all civil cases in India.

- The average time taken to resolve a property dispute, from creation of the dispute to resolution by the Supreme Court, is 20 years.

2.2 Types of property cases

Property and land disputes encompass a wide variety of cases in Indian courts. In this section we look at a few types of property cases.

2.2.1 Property cases related to succession

Cases related to succession and inheritance (especially concerning the Hindu Succession Act 1925) encompass a good percentage of the pending property cases in Indian courts. These can encompass cases related to probating the will of the person, or division of the property among legal heirs in absence of a will and so on.

Usually, such cases start when the patriarch or matriarch of a joint family dies and the siblings or other relatives fight each other to gain a larger share of the property left by the deceased person.

2.2.2 Property cases related to registration of land records

Some of the property cases occur when a buyer buys some property and finds out it is not registered properly with the land authorities or municipal authorities by the previous owners. It is then a painstaking process to prove that they are the owners and get the property registered in their names.

There are rules related to which land is allocated for agriculture, which for residential areas and which for industry, and rules on how to petition for conversion of land use. If such rules are violated, then again proving the legality of the property is a difficult process.

Registering a property in many states of India is a difficult process, involving things like giving bribes to the municipal authorities.

Sometimes the builders of an apartment complex or villa may have not done the construction of part of the flats in an authorized manner as per the rules of the municipality. There are a number of complex rules related to how much boundary to keep, what is the size of balcony and common areas, how much parking space is allocated and so on, which may be broken during construction and can lead to problems in getting the property legalized.

2.2.3 Property cases due to fraud and other crimes

Some of the ongoing property cases may be related to fraudulent transactions, such as when a person has been fraudulently deprived of their rightful claim on the land or property. There can also be other crimes involved, such as forcing a person to give up their property rights using threats and intimidation.

2.2.4 Property cases due to tenancy

Some of the cases may be due to a tenant refusing to vacate their land when their tenancy period has expired. The landlord would be forced to fight a case for many years to get back the possession of their own property, while the tenant continued to enjoy their stay.

2.2.5 Property cases due to trespassing or illegal occupation

Some of the property cases may be related to trespassing or illegal occupation of part or whole of the property. It could be by a relative or a neighbor or even a stranger. This can be the case where the original owner has been away for a while and the opposite party has encroached on their property or made unauthorized construction on the property. This is a common problem in case of Non Resident Indians (NRIs), who might be away for some years and working in a foreign country and unable to monitor their property closely.

In property cases, the rule seems to be that "possession is king". Whoever has already got possession of the property, whether by legal means or by hook or crook, it is an uphill task to dislodge them by the courts.

On top of this, rules such as "adverse possession" after 12 years give an incentive for people to knowingly trespass on someone else's land for hope of getting it after 12 years.

2.3 Complexities of the law related to property

One problem is lots of exceptions in the law and the complexities of the cases. There are a number of laws related to inheritance, such as Indian Succession act, 1925. There are different variances in the succession laws for Muslims and Christians and Hindus.

There are also a number of exceptions and special clauses in various laws, for example in states like Uttaranchal, Himachal Pradesh and North East, where only people who are domiciled are allowed to own land.

This creates a situation where there are too many laws and a common man has no choice but to take the help of expensive lawyers and court cases to enforce their property rights using the applicable laws.

2.4 Economic Inequality and Access to Justice

Litigation costs create structural inequality. Wealthy litigants can strategically delay cases, while poorer parties often abandon legitimate claims due to cost, uncertainty, and limited legal literacy.

2.5 How to lower the number of property cases

In this section, we discuss a few ways in which the number of pending property related cases can be reduced.

Some of the ways to reduce the number and time of resolution of property cases are as follows:

- Courts can upgrade the infrastructure to have more virtual hearings rather than physical hearings. These can be facilitated by widely available online meeting software such as Zoom, Google meet, Microsoft teams or Cisco Webex. This will reduce the need for unnecessary travel by the litigants.

- The Government can amend and simplify the property related laws. This would clarify confusion and thus reduce the need for pending cases. They can reduce the number of exceptions and special cases in property related laws and try to make the laws uniform across India.

- Courts can better facilitate the opposite parties to mediate and resolve the disputes themselves. Although such mechanisms with court appointed mediators currently exist, they may not always be effective in reaching an agreement.

- Courts can further encourage mechanisms like lok adalats to more efficiently resolve property related disputes, and thus reduce the burden on regular courts.

- High courts and supreme court can publish a few guidelines and best practices that might facilitate the speedy resolutions of property disputes.

- The courts can define some maximum length of time within which a judgment must be made in property related cases

- Courts can prioritize long pending property disputes.

- The government can act to reduce corruption in government bodies such as city municipalities, land registration offices and the police. This alone can reduce the number of pending property cases.

- Courts can introduce some ways to make judges accountable. Or else, they can experiment with alternative kinds of judgment such as a jury system, which is common in some countries like USA.

- Courts can institute processes to give speedier interim relief in some kinds of property disputes, such as trespass related cases.

- The government can help with the digitalization of land records and regularization of property records such as A-katha and B-katha in Karnataka state. This would make it easier to determine who are the rightful owners of any property.

References

1. Thomas Reuters, Deccan Chronicle. Millions of land, property cases stuck in courts. August 2016. Available: https://www.deccanchronicle.com/nation/current-affairs/090816/millions-of-land-property-cases-stuck-in-indian-courts.html

2. Namita Wahi, Center for Policy Research. Understanding Land Conflict in India and Suggestions for Reform. June 2019. Available: https://cprindia.org/news/7922

3. Arunav Kaul, Ahmed Pathan, Harish Narasappa. Daksh report. Deconstructing Delay: Analyses of Data from High Courts and Subordinate Courts. Available: https://dakshindia.org/Daksh_Justice_in_India/19_chapter_01.xhtml

Chapter 3: Delays in criminal cases

In this chapter, we consider the delays in criminal cases and ways in which to fix the same. Delays in criminal cases are even more serious than delays in civil cases because the person's liberty, which is enshrined in the Indian constitution, is at stake. Therefore, it is even more important to clear the backlogs in case of criminal cases.

3.1 Number of ongoing criminal cases

A report in Bloomberg Quint found that 33% of the unresolved high court cases were criminal cases. In district and subordinate courts, however, the majority of pending cases were criminal, 2.5 crore out of 3.4 crore.

3.2 High number of undertrials in Indian jails

As mentioned earlier in section 1.3, based on a 2020 Hindu report and NCRB report, there are high numbers of undertrials languishing in Indian jails, which is about double the number of those convicted of actual crimes. This is also shown in the graph in figure 5.

The same report also showed that the period of confinement of undertrials has also been increasing steadily year by year, between 2000 and 2019. Most of the undertrials have less education, 90% were not graduates, and 28% are illiterate. This makes it difficult for them to fight for their rights and obtain a speedy release from jail.

Such undertrials are often too poor to afford bail or to hire an expensive lawyer to fight their cases. This could be one of the factors in their longer periods of confinement.

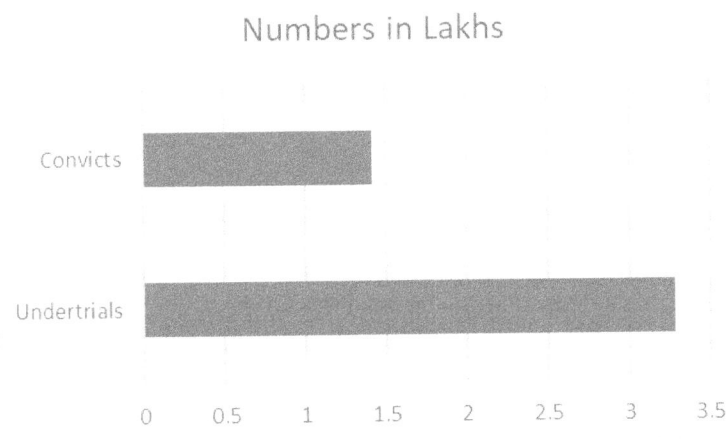

Figure: Graph showing the absolute number of convicts and undertrials in India, as per a 2019 report in Hindu newspaper

3.3 Problem with long pending criminal cases

Unlike civil cases, the litigants in criminal cases can go to jail. In cases of undertrials they are already in jail even though their guilt is not yet proved. This in itself presents a problem in the denial of liberty and denial of justice. The recent death of Stan Swamy while in judicial custody, who was a high-profile octogenarian and social worker, further highlighted this situation.

On top of this, the unhygienic conditions, bad food and medical facilities in Indian jails often make the confinement itself unpleasant and does nothing to integrate the criminals back into society.

3.4 Some recommendations to reduce the number of criminal cases

In order to reduce the number of pending criminal cases, some of the ways are as follows:

- Make more criminal cases bailable.

- Make the bail process simplified and smoother. In some cases, allow bail hearings to be held virtually.

- Urgently clear the backlog of criminal cases on a priority basis.

- Where the undertrials accused of minor crimes are languishing in jail simply because they cannot afford a lawyer or pay the bail fees, the bail can be paid by the government or waived off completely.

- Devise a system to provide incentives to judges, police and government agencies to complete a speedier investigation and disposal of criminal cases.

- Make the disposal of certain types of criminal cases time bound.

- In case a criminal case is found to be based on false accusations, institute procedures to penalize the false accusers in order to deter such filing of false criminal cases.

- Conduct research into the socio economic factors related to crime, and devise a system that emphasizes re-integration into society rather than punishment.

3.5 Undertrials and the Erosion of Liberty

A large majority of Indian prisoners are undertrials. Delays transform pre-trial detention into de facto punishment, disproportionately harming marginalized communities and eroding public trust.

3.6 Conclusion

In this chapter, we discussed the pending numbers of criminal cases, especially in lower courts, the high number of undertrials, and ways in which this can be reduced.

References

1. National Crime Research Bureau (NCRB) report. Crime in India 2020. Available: https://ncrb.gov.in/en/Crime-in-India-2020

2. Bloomberg Quint. India's pending court cases on the rise: In charts. 29 September 2020. Available: https://www.bloombergquint.com/law-and-policy/indias-pending-court-cases-on-the-rise-in-charts

3. Vignesh Radhakrishnan and Sumant Sen, the Hindu. 70% prisoners in India are undertrials. Sep 2020. Available: https://www.thehindu.com/data/data-70-prisoners-in-india-are-undertrials/article32569643.ece

4. Nandita Rao, Indian Express. For India's undertrials, the legal process is the punishment. July 2021. Available: https://indianexpress.com/article/opinion/columns/for-indias-undertrials-the-legal-process-is-the-punishment-7411017/

Chapter 4: Delays in court cases related to family disputes

Family disputes, especially marital disputes, are another large category of pending court cases. Such cases include divorce cases, cases related to issues such as domestic violence, dowry, child custody, alimony, maintenance and so on. In this chapter, we discuss such cases and some ways in which to reduce them or resolve the pending cases quicker.

4.1 Number of pending family and divorce cases

The number of divorce cases and cases related to other family and marital disputes has been slowly increasing each year. As per a 2020 article in the new Indian express, the number of fresh divorce cases filed in Indian courts in a single city, Kochi, was 3122 in 2019, which was higher than previous years.

Delays in Court Cases in India

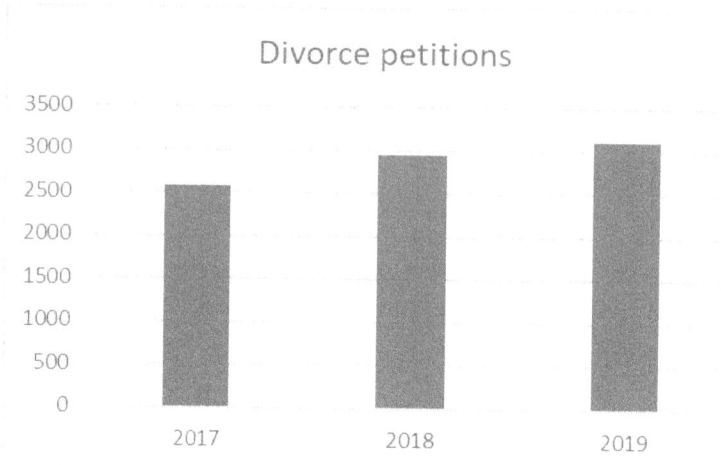

Figure: Graph showing the number of fresh divorce petitions filed each year in the city of Kochi, Kerala from 2017-2019

Another report in Hindustan times for Mumbai said the number of divorce petitions was between 7500 to 8300 for each year between 2011 and 2019. In the subsequent Covid-19 pandemic related lockdown of 2020, the numbers came down to 5059 petitions but is expected to recover to previous levels.

Another kind of major matrimonial case is related to the IPC 498a or anti dowry act. The National Crime Records Bureau data showed that the number of 498a cases was 125298 in 2019, an increase of 21.3% compared to 2018.

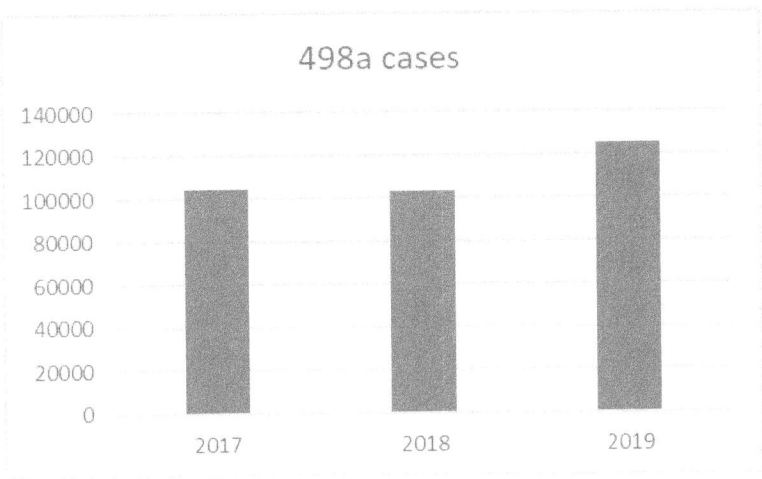

Figure: Graph showing the number of fresh 498a cases filed in India from 2017-2019

The study by Daksh found that about 14% of surveyed people were involved in family disputes, making it a major source of civil litigation after property cases.

Many or most of the pending cases related to family disputes are marital disputes between estranged husbands and wives. Divorce cases, especially the disputed divorce cases rather than mutual consent divorce, typically go on for years. Similar is the situation with other such cases such as child custody or domestic violence.

4.2 Problems with long pending family cases

One of the problems with long pending family cases is that they are unproductive and a drain on the economy, and not to the benefit of any party in the long run. If one party in a marriage wants a divorce, the marriage is already broken even if the other party does not want it. Dragging the divorce court case does not benefit anyone. Rather, they are a drain on the resources of both parties who have to pay their respective lawyers till the time the case is running. Often, the best and prime years of the life of the husband and wife are lost fighting these cases.

Often one marriage breakdown ends up in multiple marital cases, such as 498a, DV, maintenance under Hindu marriage act 1955, child custody cases and so on. Sometimes, these cases can be running in different cities. This causes unnecessary costs and hardship for the litigants who have to travel for each court date.

Another problem is that of false allegations and misuse of anti-dowry laws by estranged wives to implicate the entire family of the husband. An article in iPleaders flagged the phenomenon of high number of 498a cases with a very low conviction rate, presumably because some or most of them might have been false cases. High courts and supreme court have made statements against the misuse of the provisions of IPC 498a. The film "Martyrs of marriage" by Deepika Bhardwaj also highlighted the plight of those who are trapped in such cases.

4.3 Suggestions to reduce the number and duration of family cases

Some of the ways to reduce the number of pending family cases are as follows:

- Introduce a time bound provision for disposal of family cases, especially divorce cases and 498a.

- In case of allegations being proved false in criminal marital cases, introduce strict penalties for the persons making the false allegations. This would deter such false cases in the long run.

- Introduce better and quicker provisions for mediation in marital disputes, led by qualified people

- Research and if needed, amend the family laws, in case of high incidence of misuse.

- Increase the number of family counselling centers to provide free counselling to couples who need it.

- Make clear and simple laws which take a holistic view of all aspects of marital disputes including shared child custody, payment of alimony, civil and criminal cases and divorce cases and so on. All of these aspects should be part of the same court case.

- Make provisions so that one marriage breakdown does not lead to multiple court cases.

4.4 Conclusion

In this chapter, we have discussed the court cases related to family disputes, specifically marital disputes such as divorce, child custody, maintenance and 498a. Here too the laws need to be rationalized and simplified to reduce the number of ongoing cases.

References

1. The new Indian express. Divorce pleas hit a record 3,122 in 2019. Jan 2020. Available: https://www.newindianexpress.com/cities/kochi/2020/jan/28/divorce-pleas-hit-a-record-3122-in-2019-2095352.html

2. Charul Shah, Hindustan Times. Mumbai reported an average of 22 divorce petitions daily. Jan 2021. Available: https://www.hindustantimes.com/cities/others/mumbai-reported-an-average-of-22-divorce-petitions-daily-101612038442268.html

3. Ambika Pandit, Times of India. Parliament panel highlights huge variation in number of cases under domestic violence law and IPC provisions on 'cruelty by husband'. Mar 2021. Available: http://timesofindia.indiatimes.com/articleshow/81624225.cms

4. Ayush Verma, iPleaders. Misuse of Section 498A under IPC. August 2020. Available: https://blog.ipleaders.in/misuse-section-498a-ipc/

5. Padmini Baruah, Shruthi Naik, Surya Prakash B.S., Kishore Mandyam, Daksh Report. Paths to Justice: Surveying Judicial and Non-judicial Dispute Resolution in India. Available: https://dakshindia.org/Daksh_Justice_in_India/12_chapter_02.xhtml

6. Hindustan Times. Section 498-A being misused to implicate husband's entire family: Bombay high court. Oct 2020. Available: https://www.hindustantimes.com/mumbai-news/section-498-a-being-misused-to-implicate-husband-s-entire-family-bombay-high-court/story-SJAdXS3OuXtXiq0Qx2IVDO.html

Chapter 5: Problem of lack of judges

One of the big reasons for the high number of pending court cases in India is lack of judges and insufficient infrastructure in the courts, especially the lower courts. In this chapter we discuss this problem and suggest some ways to fix the same.

5.1 Number of judges and the recruitment gap

A number of judicial personalities such as chief justices of India and various law commissions have complained about the lack of judges and the need for speedier recruitment of judges to clear the backlog of pending court cases.

India has only less than 17000 judges in total, with 17 judges per million of the population, which is probably the lowest judge to population ratio in the world.

The ideal number should be around 60000 judges for the 50 judges per million ratio, as per the findings of the law commission of India.

A 2016 report in Mint quoted the then Chief Justice Thakur as stating that India needs 70000 more judges to clear the backlog. Else with the current strength, the backlog will take more than 300 years to clear. These numbers would have only increased since then.

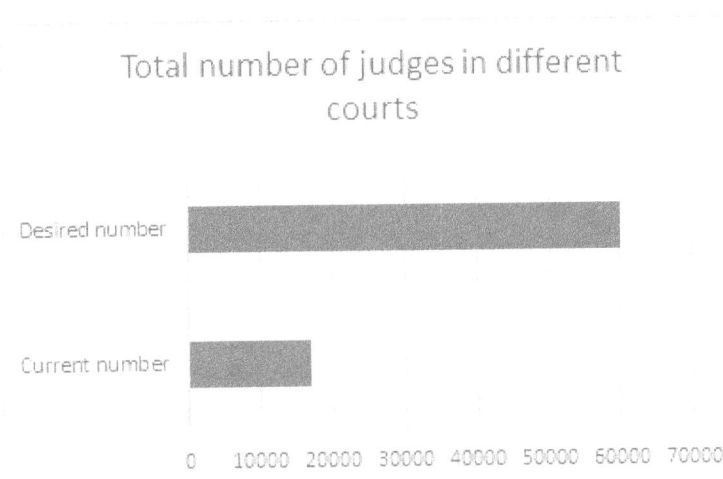

Figure: Graph showing the desired vs current number of judges in India.

5.2 Delays in recruitment of judges

New judicial recruitments are also not being done soon enough. The government is also not doing enough to recruit the needed increased number of judges. There is a high standard needed for recruitment of judges, especially on recruitment of judges to higher courts such as high court and supreme court.

Even today, thousands of vacancies (up to one third of the sanctioned strength, which itself is low) are lying unfilled. As per a report in Hindu newspaper, even the Supreme Court and high courts (455 judicial vacancies against a sanctioned strength of 1098) have a high number of unfilled vacancies.

The budget allocated by the government for the judiciary infrastructure is low as well.

5.3 Too many court holidays

A 2018 report in Bloomberg Quint stated that the Supreme court was functional for 193 days a year, high courts for only 210 days a year and subordinate courts for 245 days a year on average. There are a number of government holidays, festival holidays, summer and winter breaks and so on, that results in courts closing for the vacations. This could be another factor in the long pendency of court cases. If the number of holidays is rationalized, the courts would be able to clear the backlog faster.

5.4 Conclusion

In this chapter, we discussed the problems of lack of judges, slow recruitment and too many court holidays as contributing factors in the high pendency of court cases in India. Only a concerted effort on the part of the government and judiciary to increase recruitments and make the courts more efficient can solve the issues.

References

1. Alok Prasanna Kumar, Mint. July 2016. How many judges does India really need? Available: https://www.livemint.com/Politics/3B97SMGhseobYhZ6qpAYoN/How-many-judges-does-India-really-need.html

2. Krishnadas Rajgopal, the Hindu. August 2021. Rising judicial vacancies a challenge to Supreme Court Collegium. Available: https://www.thehindu.com/news/national/rising-judicial-vacancies-a-challenge-to-sc-collegium/article35926889.ece

3. Arvind Kumar, the Print. October 2020. Over one-third of judges' posts lie vacant in 12 high courts. So much for collegiums. Available: https://theprint.in/opinion/one-third-judges-posts-lie-vacant-in-12-high-courts-so-much-for-collegiums/532266/

4. Sayan Ghosal, Business Standard. Why India's courts are struggling to find judges. Jan 2020. Available: https://www.business-standard.com/article/specials/why-india-s-courts-are-struggling-to-find-judges-116061600898_1.html

5. Siddharth Mandrekar Rao, the Print. Will increasing number of courts aid India's judicial backlog? Data shows otherwise. Dec 2020. Available: https://theprint.in/opinion/will-increasing-number-of-courts-aid-indias-judicial-backlog-data-shows-otherwise/571224/

6. Harish Narasappa, Bloomberg Quint. Court Vacations: Are They Justified? Dec 2018. Available: https://www.bloombergquint.com/opinion/court-vacations-are-they-justified

Chapter 6: Delays by police and government agencies

One of the contributing factors for delays in course cases is inaction or slow action by government agencies such as the police. In this chapter, we discuss this aspect in detail.

6.1 Low confidence of the public in the police

A 2019 survey published in Times of India found that only 25% of Indians trusted the police.

A 2017 Access to Justice survey by Daksh found that 40% Indians surveyed said they would not approach the police if they had a dispute, rather preferring to go to family, friends and community elders. An additional 32% did not want to approach a lawyer either. 44% said they approached the police to file a complaint at some time but their complaint was not registered. Among the reasons the police gave for not registering an FIR immediately was that the police wanted them to compromise with the opposite party (37%) and the police did not believe them (21%).

Hence, it is clear that the confidence of public in the police is not high, because of their having bad experiences with the police not believing them or otherwise refusing to register an FIR and conduct an investigation.

6.2 Corruption of police and other government agencies

As per the findings of the Daksh survey, police often refuse to file FIRs, or refuse to investigate properly on time. They might sometimes also ask for bribes in order to register the FIR.

A study by Transparency International India in 2005 found that corruption is rampant at every level of public services in India and police stand out high on the corruption index, followed by the lower judiciary and the land administration. It reported that 92% Indians had first hand experience of paying bribes to get services performed in as public office.

If complaints are investigated promptly by the police and action is taken speedily, this could lead to disposal in the earliest stages of the cases and reduce the need for them to come to the courts, reducing the burden on the justice system. Instead, due to their inaction, cases get further delayed.

6.3 Causes of the police not taking speedy action

Why do the police and other government agencies not take speedy action in case of complaints or investigations related to ongoing court cases? This could be due to a number of factors such as the following:

- Lethargy of the police, or simply reluctance to file cases, since it would mean more work for them.
- Corruption by the police, where some of the parties are well connected politically or willing to pay bribes to get their work done.
- There could be inaction or slow action by other government agencies as well.
- The police may be more hesitant to take action if the complainants are poor, not politically connected, or from rural areas.

6.4 Conclusion

In this chapter, we have seen how the confidence in the police by the Indian public is low. The police are often reluctant to file FIRs and act on complaints. Corruption might also be present in case of police and other government agencies. All this results in a situation where slow or shoddy investigation further delays the ongoing court cases.

References

1. Times of India. Only 25% Indians trust police: Survey. Nov 2019. Available: https://timesofindia.indiatimes.com/india/only-25-indians-trust-police-survey/articleshow/72302944.cms

2. Padmini Baruah, Shruthi Naik, Surya Prakash B.S., Kishore Mandyam, Daksh Report. Paths to Justice: Surveying Judicial and Non-judicial Dispute Resolution in India. Available: https://dakshindia.org/Daksh_Justice_in_India/12_chapter_02.xhtml

3. Transparency International India, Center for Media studies. India corruption study. 2005. Available: https://web.archive.org/web/20130811123343/http://www.iri.org.in/related_readings/India%20Corruption%20Study%202005.pdf

Chapter 7: Intentional delays by litigants

All court case delays are not just due to lack of judges or such factors. Sometimes, the litigants themselves might be responsible for delaying the court cases due to various kinds of motivation. This may include filing frivolous cases and other delaying tactics. In this chapter, we discuss some of the ways and reasons for the same.

7.1 Motivation for litigants to delay cases

Litigants can have various motivations to delay the cases. For example, if one party are illegally occupying the other party's property, they may want the justice to be delayed in order to keep staying on the property.

Similarly, if one party is accused of a criminal offence, they may be motivated to delay the case so that they do not have to bear the punishment for the crime for as long as possible.

7.2 Filing of frivolous cases

The filing of frivolous cases by one party upon another is one of the common ways in which legislation delays can occur. The party filing the frivolous cases knows very well they are unlikely to win and will be eventually defeated, yet they file such cases with the hopes of delaying the main case or putting pressure on the other party and force them to come to compromise by harassing them.

Judges of the Supreme Courts and high courts have themselves complained about such cases on multiple occasions.

The Supreme Court in 2021 regretted that scores of "frivolous" matters have been making it "dysfunctional". They made the remark while hearing a consumer dispute case, which was wrapped up by the court in March but a fresh application was filed in the same matter. Justice Chandrachud observed that the final order had already been issued in terms of what the petitioner wanted, but he chose to come back with a trivial issue.

In Subrata Roy Sahara v. Union of India, (2014) 8 SCC 470, Justice Khehar made the following observations:

"The Indian judicial system is grossly afflicted, with frivolous litigation. Ways and means need to be evolved, to deter litigants from their compulsive obsession, towards senseless and ill-considered claims. One needs to keep in mind, that in the process of litigation, there is an innocent sufferer on the other side, of every irresponsible and senseless claim. He suffers long drawn anxious periods of nervousness and restlessness, whilst the litigation is pending, without any fault on his part. He

pays for the litigation, from out of his savings (or out of his borrowings), worrying that the other side may trick him into defeat, for no fault of his. He spends invaluable time briefing counsel and preparing them for his claim. Time which he should have spent at work, or with his family, is lost, for no fault of his. Should a litigant not be compensated for, what he has lost, for no fault?...

Does the concerned litigant realize, that the litigant on the other side has had to defend himself, from Court to Court, and has had to incur expenses towards such defence? And there are some litigants who continue to pursue senseless and ill-considered claims, to somehow or the other, defeat the process of law. ..."

7.3 Techniques by litigants to intentionally delay their ongoing court cases

The different techniques by which the litigants themselves can delay the cases can include the following:

- Not being present during some of the court dates

- Inserting unnecessary applications and petitions in the ongoing court case to divert the court's attention

- Asking for repeated adjournments on multiple dates

- Requesting the court for information from banks or other government agencies, in order to further delay the progress of the case while such information is procured.

- Refusing to cooperate with the execution, even after the court order has been given.

- Unnecessary or frivolous appeals to higher courts.

- Filing multiple frivolous cases in order to delay the original case and to harass the opposite parties.

- Twisting some of the opposite party statements and alleging perjury on that basis.

7.4 How to reduce delays by litigants

The way to control such delays by the litigants is as follows: Judges at all levels need to be trained to be vigilant to tactics by any of the litigating parties to delay their ongoing cases, by filing frivolous cases or any other ways, and should strictly penalize any attempts at creating such delays.

The system has to be redesigned in such a way that this kind of tactics are disincentivized. Particularly, potential frivolous cases should be stopped at the filing stage itself.

Once the litigants realize that these delaying tactics are not working, they would automatically stop them and the pending cases can get speeded up.

7.5 Conclusion

In this chapter we discussed a few ways in which the litigants themselves might delay the ongoing cases, due to vested motivations. All of these techniques can individually or collectively delay the progress of the cases by wasting the time of the courts, and result in the overall slow disposal of cases.

References:

1. Utkarsh Anand, Hindustan Times. Jun 1, 2021. Frivolous cases making SC dysfunctional: Justice Chandrachud. Available: https://www.hindustantimes.com/india-news/frivolous-cases-making-sc-dysfunctional-justice-chandrachud-101622534333467.html

Chapter 8: Public Interest Litigation (PILs)

Cases such as Public Interest Litigation (PILs), although made with good intention, also cause an increase in the number of court cases, further overburdening the system. In this chapter we discuss such cases.

8.1 Origin and intention of PILs

PILs are intended to enable the raising of certain issues of social importance that affect a number of people in society, especially in cases where the rights of one or more underprivileged groups are being denied. The first PIL was filed in 1979 by advocate Kapila Hingorani on behalf of prisoners languishing in Bihar jails, a landmark moment that opened the doors of the Supreme Court to citizens who could not otherwise afford representation. These can be filed in the high courts and supreme court under articles 32 and 226 of the Constitution of India.

PILs have been responsible for some of the most significant judicial interventions in India's history. Environmental pollution, child labour, bonded labour, rehabilitation of displaced persons, and conditions in prisons and mental asylums have all been improved as a result of PIL proceedings. The Vishaka guidelines on sexual harassment at the workplace, which later formed the basis of the POSH Act, were the outcome of a PIL. In this respect, PILs represent a powerful democratic tool, one that gives ordinary citizens and civil society organisations a means to hold the government and public institutions accountable before the highest courts.

8.2 Misuse of PILs

However, the concept of PIL can be abused by some parties for their own vested interests, including political interests.

This can be done by filing frivolous PILs, with the intention of getting publicity, political rivalry or for delaying ongoing court cases.

The 2021 report in iPleaders found that PILs can sometimes be used as a tool for harassment.

Some examples of how PILs can be misused include the following. A competitor in business might file a PIL against a company alleging environmental violations, not because of genuine concern but to delay a project or cause financial damage. Politicians have used PILs to challenge administrative decisions that affect their rivals, thereby converting a judicial mechanism into a tool of political warfare. In some cases, petitioners have filed PILs seeking directions on matters that are clearly within the domain of the executive or legislature, effectively using the courts to bypass democratic processes. The Supreme Court and various high courts have expressed frustration with such petitions on multiple occasions, noting that the time spent on them comes directly at the cost of genuine cases waiting for hearings.

8.3 Suggestions to reduce PIL misuse

Courts and legislators can take the following steps to reduce the misuse of PILs while preserving the mechanism for genuine public interest causes: Introduce a preliminary screening stage where a bench examines whether a PIL meets minimum standards of public interest before admitting it. Impose meaningful costs on petitioners who file frivolous PILs, as the Supreme Court has occasionally done. Require that PILs be accompanied by an affidavit verifying the factual basis of the petition. Restrict repeated filing by the same petitioner on closely related issues once a petition has been dismissed. Ensure that courts hearing PILs are guided by clear principles distinguishing genuine public interest from private or political grievance dressed in public interest language.

8.4 Conclusion

In this chapter, we discussed how PILs originated as a vital tool for social justice and have yielded landmark improvements in the lives of ordinary citizens. However, the same mechanism can be misused to burden courts with frivolous or politically motivated petitions. Striking the right balance, preserving PIL as a genuine instrument of accountability while firmly discouraging its misuse, is essential if courts are to keep their dockets manageable and serve real justice efficiently.

References

1. Diva Rai and Manya Dudeja, iPleaders. Abuse of the concept of PIL in recent years with examples of case laws. June 2021. Available: https://blog.ipleaders.in/abuse-of-the-concept-of-pil-in-recent-years-with-examples-of-case-laws/

Chapter 9: Recommendations to speed up court cases

In the previous chapters, we have discussed various reasons for delays in court cases in India. In this chapter, we discuss some ways to fix the delays and speed up the time taken to get verdicts.

9.1 Use of technology

One important way to speed up ongoing court cases is use of technology and its infinite possibilities.

For example, natural language processing (NLP) and artificial intelligence (AI) / Machine Learning (ML) tools can be used in the following ways:

- To identify the salient points in court petitions. AI/ML tools can be used to identify and annotate from the petition the basic facts of the case, the evidence placed and the prayer. This can help to prepare a summary of the salient points in the case, presented in an annotated form. This can aid the judges in understanding the petitions and in delivering verdicts faster and more accurately.

- AI/ML tools can be used to search references of similar cases and verdicts, from a database of past cases. This can help both litigants and lawyers to better prepare their cases. This can also help the judges to deliver more balanced verdicts that take previous relevant case law into consideration.

- By training ML models on a dataset of past cases, and using this to predict the verdicts in ongoing cases on the basis of similarity with past cases. This can help the judges to make more consistent and correct decisions.

- To identify and dismiss frivolous cases at the time of filing, based on certain criteria or by prediction using ML models trained on legal data. This can save the courts and the litigants time and money.

- In some types of minor cases, AI/ML tools can be used to resolve the cases online without the litigants having to come to the court at all. This can help to save effort, time and money for all the parties.

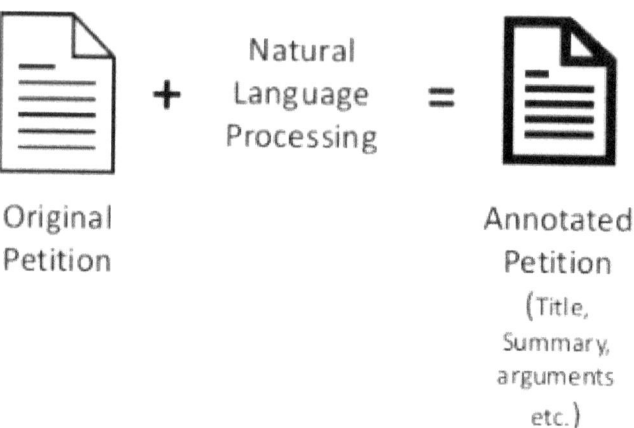

Figure: Use of Natural Language Processing (NLP) tools to annotate court petitions and help the judge reach faster and more accurate verdicts.

Technology can also be utilized to fully digitize the filing of cases, to have virtual hearings and to update the results of each hearing digitally on the court website. The e-courts system is a good example of this, although its adoption is not uniform across India, especially for the lower courts.

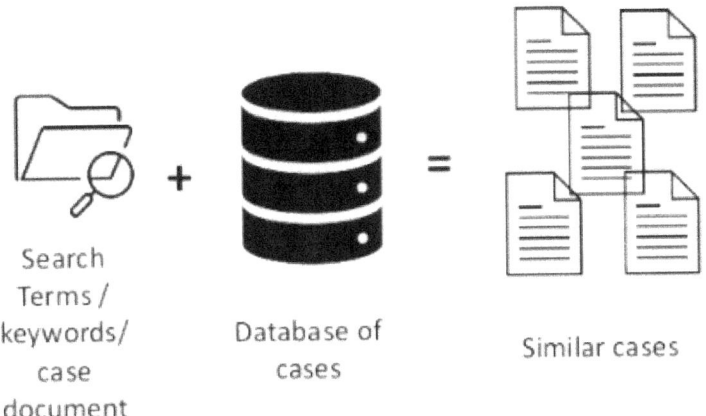

Figure: Use of AI/ML technologies to search similar cases and verdicts to the current case being considered.

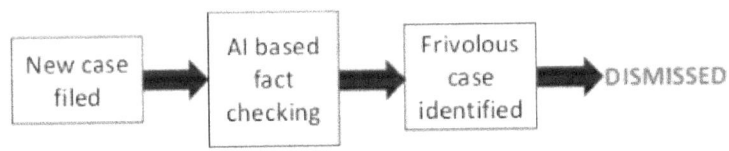

Figure: Use of AI/ML to perform basic fact checking on new petitions to identify and dismiss frivolous cases at the time of filing.

Delays in Court Cases in India

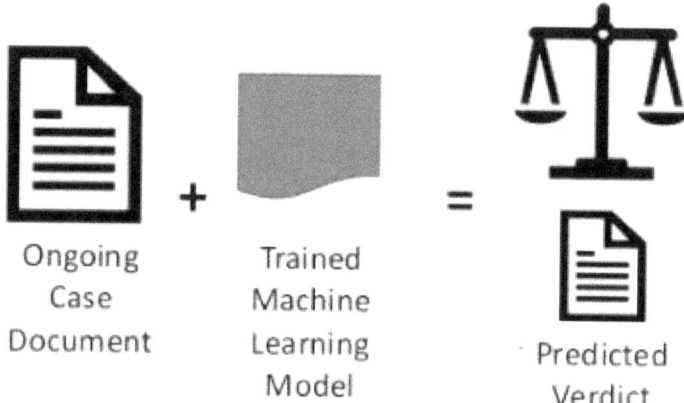

Figure: Use of AI/ML models to predict the verdicts of ongoing court cases and thus help the judges to give more accurate verdicts.

All such steps, such as virtual hearings and digitalization of each step of the court process, have the potential to save the time of the courts, litigants, lawyers and judges, make the court process more efficient, as well as reduce the possibilities for misuse of the process and wasting time of the courts.

However, it is also important to be judicious in the use of technology, based on gradually transitioning to a hybrid system and then after a trial period fully adopting the new virtual system. Technology adoption needs to be holistic and it is important to be sure of the intentions behind it, rather than jumping too fast to move to a virtual mode.

Courts and policy makers can take cues from how technology is used in courts around the world, especially in developed countries.

9.1.1 Predictive Policing and Its Risks

In some countries, police have begun using computer models to "predict" where crime will happen or who might be involved in it. These systems are meant to help the police act faster, but they often repeat past biases. If an area was heavily policed earlier, the model again marks the same area as "high risk," even if nothing new has changed. Such systems can unfairly target certain neighbourhoods or communities.

If India ever considers similar tools, it must proceed very carefully. A biased policing model will only increase wrongful arrests and unnecessary criminal cases, adding even more pressure to the courts. Technology should support fair investigation, not reinforce old prejudices.

9.1.2 Algorithmic Bail and Decision Support

Some American courts use computer programs to help judges decide bail or sentencing. These tools estimate whether an accused person is likely to reoffend or skip trial. Although they are meant to make decisions more consistent, they have been criticised for being biased against poorer or minority groups.

India does not use such tools today, but as our systems become more digital, the idea may come up in the future. Bail is one of the biggest causes of delay in criminal courts, and some may think algorithms can help. But such tools should never replace a judge's independent mind. Any technology used in bail matters must be transparent and used only as a rough guide, not as a final decision-maker.

9.1.3 AI-Assisted Drafting of Orders

Several courts abroad, including in China and parts of Europe, now use AI software to prepare first drafts of routine orders or summaries of long case bundles. Judges then review and correct these drafts. This saves time on clerical tasks and helps courts dispose of cases faster. Some Indian High Courts have begun experimenting with AI-generated summaries. This can speed up work, but judges must always verify the content. AI sometimes makes mistakes or invents incorrect citations. Technology must remain an assistant, not an author.

9.1.4 AI Tools for Digital Evidence and Authentication

More and more evidence today is digital, such as videos, audio clips, screenshots, messages and CCTV footage. With generative AI tools, it is now possible to create fake videos or audio recordings that look real. This is a challenge for the courts.

To deal with this, some countries are using AI forensic tools that can detect manipulated files by analysing metadata or tiny visual distortions. India will also need strong digital forensic support so that judges can be confident that the evidence presented before them is genuine. Without this, courts may see rising disputes about authenticity, leading to further delays.

9.1.5 Deepfakes as a New Threat

Deepfake technology allows anyone to create a video where a person appears to say or do something they never did. Such fake material can be used to file false criminal cases, influence family disputes, or confuse investigations.

Courts will need clear rules for verifying video and audio evidence. Chain-of-custody procedures, digital fingerprinting, and forensic checks must become standard. This is essential to prevent misuse and protect innocent people from fabricated evidence.

9.1.6 Use of Large Language Models (LLMs)

Large Language Models are a recent development in artificial intelligence and can support the courts in several practical ways when used carefully. These models can read long documents, identify relevant issues, and generate concise summaries. They can also assist lawyers and judges by organising facts, extracting timelines, and preparing readable drafts of routine orders or notices, which can then be checked and finalised by human officers.

LLMs can also help litigants who cannot afford expensive legal assistance by guiding them through basic procedural steps, explaining legal terminology in simple language, and helping them draft applications or responses more clearly. They may also be used to improve the quality of legal aid services by analysing case bundles faster and identifying what information is missing.

Another use of LLMs is in managing large collections of judgments. These models can group similar cases, highlight relevant precedents, and surface contradictions or overlaps between different rulings. This can save significant time during research and help ensure consistent application of the law.

However, LLMs must always remain advisory tools. They sometimes make factual errors or misinterpret legal context, and they cannot understand human circumstances or apply judicial discretion. Their output must always be reviewed, verified, and corrected by trained legal professionals or judges. Used carefully, LLMs can reduce clerical burden and improve access to information, while keeping the final responsibility for every decision firmly in human hands.

9.2 AI Ethics in Judicial Use

As the judiciary uses more technology, ethical safeguards become as important as the technology itself. Courts must ensure that no digital system, whether used for search, summarising, prediction, or evidence analysis, violates fairness, transparency or accountability.

Litigants should know when AI has been used in their case. Judges must rely on AI only for assistance, never as the final authority. Any tool used must be explainable, meaning its reasoning can be understood if questioned. Models based on biased data must be avoided, as they can produce biased outcomes at scale. Above all, responsibility for every judicial decision must remain with human judges. Technology can support justice, but it must not become an excuse for errors or unfairness.

9.3 Recruit more judges

As mentioned in previous chapters, one of the current issues is that there are currently a large number of vacancies for judges in various courts. Also, the ratio of judges to the population is much less than the desired ratio of 50 judges per million of population.

Hence, one obvious solution to this problem is to recruit more judges in an urgent basis until the desired number is reached. The recruitment must also be complemented with proper training and sensitization of the judges.

9.4 Improve the court infrastructure

The court infrastructure needs to be improved in order to make it more efficient and ensure the litigants have a better overall experience.

One important way in which the infrastructure can be upgraded includes the following: upgrade all the courts, especially the lower levels of courts, to enable digitalization of court records and enabling of virtual hearings.

9.5 Have time bounds on litigation

The courts need to have maximum time limits for certain kinds of litigation. This will ensure that cases do not need to drag on for years.

9.6 Reduce corruption and increase efficiency in police and other government agencies

Since some of the court delays are due to inefficient or corrupt government office, especially the police, they can be remedied only if the corruption is controlled. Police need to be strictly incentivized against bribe taking and for speedy investigation and penalized when they refuse to file FIRs in response to complaints.

9.7 Simplify the laws

Many of the court cases happen because the laws, for example in property and family matters, are too complex and have too many special cases and exceptions. This can be controlled by rationalizing and simplifying the related laws. Their implementation should be closely monitored and laws that are reported to be widely misused should be changed or abandoned.

In criminal laws, minor crimes should be made bailable and compoundable and strict guidelines regarding arrests and bail should be followed.

9.8 Detect frivolous cases and close them early

Many of the pending cases are frivolous in nature, filed with the intent to harass or other vested interests. Such cases should be screened out as early as possible to avoid burdening the court system. There should be ways to track those who repeatedly file such frivolous cases and they should be penalized in some way as well.

9.9 Have some form of accountability for judges

Currently, there is no accountability for judges who give bad judgments or do not handle the cases properly. There should be some mechanism for their accountability and oversight. In particular, judges should be incentivized to give speedy verdicts and not keep cases dragging on for a long time.

9.10 Some overall recommendations to speed up ongoing court cases

Some of the ways in which pending cases can be speeded up include the following:

- Increase the recruitment of judges at all levels. Fill up the pending gaps in recruitment as soon as possible.

- Make virtual hearings, using software on a computer, possible in all courts including lower courts (this has got some progress in recent times due to Covid-19).

- Make sure the police and other agencies do their job speedily. Introduce an element of accountability in their action.

- Increase the budget allocation from the government for judicial infrastructure.

- Improve the IT infrastructure in courts, so that cases can be heard virtually and thus disposed faster. This would reduce the need of unnecessary travel for litigants as well.

- Improve the quality of judges by better training and oversight.

- Have oversight and accountability for the judges and their verdicts. Consider alternative systems prevalent in other countries, such as a jury system.

- Institute an interim relief for the pending civil cases meeting certain pre-set criteria. The interim relief should be time bound.

- Implement the pending judicial reforms, that were suggested by the different law commissions.

- Decrease the number of court holidays

- Increase the number of courts

- Have a maximum time limit for disposal of all criminal cases, so that undertrials are not made to suffer needlessly.

- Clear the long-term pending cases on priority.

- When filing a PIL or other cases, have checks to verify if the cases are genuine or frivolous. Only cases found to be genuine shall be given a hearing.

- Apply latest technologies such as Artificial Intelligence (AI) to screen out or flag frivolous cases at the filing stage itself.

- Encourage other means for disposal for ongoing cases, such as Lok Adalats or mediated negotiation between the parties.

9.11 Conclusion

In this chapter, we have discussed some ways in which the ongoing backlog can be cleared and the court processes can be speeded up, such as by utilizing the power of technology.

References

1. Prashant Nadaraj, Outlook. Digital Courts: Are We Really Availing Infinite Possibilities Of Technology? April 2020. Available: https://www.outlookindia.com/website/story/opinion-digital-courts-are-we-really-availing-infinite-possibilities-of-technology/351800

2. E Courts Website. Available: https://ecourts.gov.in/ecourts_home/

Chapter 10: Judicial Reforms in India

India's judicial system is one of the world's largest, yet also one of the most burdened. Millions of pending cases, shortage of judges, slow processes, and outdated procedures have forced the government, courts, and policy bodies to repeatedly propose reforms. Some reforms have been implemented; many more remain on paper.

In this chapter, we discuss the key judicial reforms that have been suggested or attempted in India over the last few decades, why they matter, and what remains to be done.

10.1 Why reforms are needed

The core problems, such as case pendency, slow disposal, poor infrastructure, lack of judges, have been described earlier in this book. Judicial reforms are essentially attempts to fix these problems through changes in:

- laws
- administrative systems
- court management
- technology

- recruitment and training
- alternative dispute resolution (ADR)

India has had repeated commissions and committees examining how to improve the system. Yet the gap between the recommended reforms and the implemented reforms remains wide.

10.2 Law Commission and Early Reform Attempts

Over the last several decades, many committees, commissions and expert groups have studied the judicial system and offered recommendations.

The earliest of these came from the Law Commission of India, whose various reports repeatedly drew attention to the shortage of judges, outdated procedures, and the need for modern court management. Multiple Law Commission reports (14th, 79th, 124th, 245th, etc.) have recommended:

- Increasing judge strength
- Creating an All-India Judicial Service
- Speeding up procedure in civil and criminal trials
- Modernising court administration
- Reducing adjournments
- Using technology in courts

Later, in the 1980s and 1990s, the Arrears Committee headed by Justice V.S. Malimath highlighted the structural nature of delays and urged courts to strictly regulate adjournments and to introduce more scientific case management. Although these recommendations were widely discussed, most were implemented only partially or not at all, largely because reforms required cooperation between the judiciary, the executive, and state governments, an alignment that rarely materialised.

10.3 Reforms in early 2000s

A major wave of reform thinking began again in the early 2000s. The Malimath Committee on criminal justice emphasised victim-centric processes, better protection for witnesses, and more efficient investigation practices. Around the same time, the Law Commission revived the idea of an All-India Judicial Service, a national examination similar to the civil services, intended to create a professional, merit-based cadre of judges. The proposal has remained stuck between the Union government, state governments, and High Courts, each of whom holds a piece of constitutional authority over judicial appointments. The result is that India continues to have one of the lowest judge-to-population ratios in the world.

10.4 Technological reforms and e-courts

Technological reform entered the judicial vocabulary more seriously in the last decade. The e-Courts Mission Mode Project marked a significant change in direction by attempting to digitize case records, enable online access to cause-lists, and modernize court administration. The progress has been uneven—some high courts have moved swiftly while many subordinate courts still struggle with basic infrastructure—but the initiative has fundamentally altered how litigants experience the system. The Covid-19 pandemic unexpectedly accelerated virtual hearings, which opened up new possibilities for reducing travel, increasing efficiency, and making courts more accessible. Even so, the transition to a fully hybrid or digital system remains incomplete, with concerns about digital literacy, internet reliability, and appropriate safeguards for sensitive hearings.

10.5 Fast track courts and Mediation Act

Reforms have also taken the form of specialized courts. The creation of fast-track courts for cases involving sexual offences, commercial disputes, and motor accident claims was intended to reduce the burden of regular courts. These courts have indeed helped in certain categories, but they often inherit the same problems of vacancies, poor infrastructure, and limited administrative support. More recently, the Commercial Courts Act of 2015 attempted to introduce stricter timelines and modern dispute-resolution norms for high-value commercial matters.

The Mediation Act of 2023 further strengthened the push towards alternative dispute resolution by encouraging mediation as a first step for many civil disputes. These reforms represent a shift in thinking: litigation need not always be the default pathway to justice, especially when quicker and less adversarial options are available.

10.6 Bharatiya Nyaya Samhita and associated reforms

A substantial recent development has been the overhaul of India's criminal laws in 2023, with the introduction of the Bharatiya Nyaya Sanhita (BNS), Bharatiya Nagarik Suraksha Sanhita (BNSS), and Bharatiya Sakshya Adhiniyam (BSA). These laws aim to modernize investigation procedures, improve the handling of digital evidence, and address delays in police and prosecutorial processes. While their long-term impact is yet to be seen, they indicate a growing recognition that judicial reform cannot be isolated from reform in policing, investigation, and prosecution. A slow police investigation or badly drafted charge sheet inevitably contributes to delays in court.

10.7 Recent Reforms Underway

The years 2023 to 2025 have brought their own momentum. These are not speculative ideas but reforms in motion, many already underway, and some beginning to reshape specific parts of the justice system.

One of the most visible developments has been the rapid expansion of digitisation across courts. E-Courts Phase III, approved as a national initiative, aims not merely to computerise records but to convert the courts into largely paper-less, technology-assisted institutions. High Courts in several states have begun systematic scanning of legacy records, broad adoption of e-filing, and integration of digital cause-lists. Administrative work that earlier required physical presence: certified copies, case status checks, applications for adjournments, can now be handled online. Virtual hearings, once an emergency response to the pandemic, are increasingly accepted for certain categories of cases. Their most successful application has been the virtual court system for traffic challans and petty violations. By 2023-24, these courts in multiple states had already processed millions of cases entirely online, proving that high-volume, low-discretion matters can be disposed of without straining physical courtrooms.

Parallel to technological change is the continued expansion of fast-track courts. India's scheme for Fast Track Special Courts, originally introduced to deal with sexual offences and POCSO matters, has been extended and strengthened. Hundreds of such courts are now operational across states, and although their performance varies, the overall trend is encouraging.

Additionally, NITI Aayog has taken an increasingly active role in shaping the policy conversation around judicial efficiency. By placing law and dispute-resolution within its broader governance agenda, NITI has signalled that judicial reform is not an isolated legal issue but part of national economic and administrative planning.

10.8 Challenges to reforms

Despite these developments, many long-discussed reforms remain unrealised. The proposal for an All-India Judicial Service continues to face resistance. Court infrastructure in many states remains inadequate. Vacancies for judges, especially at the district court level, remain high, and recruitment processes are often delayed for years. The culture of frequent adjournments persists despite repeated judicial directions to curb them. Procedural laws have been amended multiple times, but their implementation varies widely between states. Technology too has its limitations: digitisation is helpful only when courts have sufficient staff and training to use the systems correctly.

Perhaps the most persistent challenge is the fragmented nature of authority. Judicial reform requires the cooperation of multiple bodies: the judiciary, which manages its own internal processes; the central government, which allocates funding and drafts legislation; the state governments, which control subordinate courts; and the bar associations, whose cooperation is essential for changes in court procedures. When even one of these actors is reluctant, otherwise promising reforms tend to stall.

10.9 Global Comparisons: Lessons from Other Justice Systems

Judicial delay is not unique to India, although its scale here is unusually large. Many countries have faced similar pressures such as growing populations, rising litigation, slow procedures, and have responded with reforms that, over time, reshaped the culture of their courts. A comparative glance does not offer simple solutions, but it does illuminate practices that have worked elsewhere and which may hold relevance for India's future.

Singapore is the most frequently cited example, not because it is wealthy or small, but because it treats judicial efficiency as a matter of national policy. There, technology is not an accessory to the judicial process but central to it. Nearly all filings are electronic; hearings in appropriate matters are conducted online; and court administrative staff are professionally trained in case management. More importantly, Singapore enforces a disciplined culture around adjournments. Judges monitor case timelines actively, and parties are expected to adhere strictly to schedules unless exceptional reasons exist. Coupled with a strong emphasis on mediation before litigation, this creates a system where disputes either settle early or proceed swiftly. For India, the lesson is not in replicating Singapore's scale but in adopting its mindset: delays are not unavoidable; they are managed.

The United Kingdom offers a different model. Its courts rely heavily on "case management conferences," where the judge actively shapes the trajectory of a case: fixing timelines, identifying issues, setting deadlines for evidence, and limiting the scope of hearings. Hearings themselves are often time-boxed, meaning that counsel must present argument within designated slots rather than extending proceedings indefinitely. The UK also uses pre-trial reviews to ensure that both sides understand the issues clearly before trial. These practices reduce uncertainty and prevent cases from meandering through procedural detours. For India, this approach underscores the value of a judge-led process in which the court takes responsibility for keeping cases on track rather than leaving scheduling to the parties.

The United States presents yet another path, shaped by its distinctive legal architecture. A large proportion of criminal cases never reach full trial because of plea bargaining, which is a negotiated admission of guilt in exchange for reduced charges or sentencing. This practice shifts the bulk of criminal justice away from courtroom adjudication and reduces the load on trial courts. Jury trials, though celebrated and constitutionally protected, are relatively rare in practice; they are reserved for the small fraction of cases that cannot be resolved by negotiation or settlement. While India cannot import the American model wholesale, the broader theme is useful: procedural mechanisms outside the traditional trial can significantly lighten a court's burden if used judiciously.

Brazil offers a compelling example for countries with scale and diversity closer to India's. Faced with chronic backlog, Brazil expanded its network of small-claims courts designed to handle low-value civil disputes swiftly and with simplified procedure. These courts use informality and accessibility to reduce litigation pressure on higher courts. Over time, Brazil also adopted various forms of online dispute resolution, enabling certain disputes to be resolved through digital platforms without requiring physical hearings. This layered system, where simple matters are handled simply, and courts are reserved for more complex disputes, has been instrumental in preventing systemic congestion.

For India, these comparisons do not imply that foreign practices can be transplanted wholesale. But they do show that sustained reform is possible. Courts can move faster; hearings can be time-bound; mediation can reduce litigation; and technology can streamline once-burdensome processes.

10.10 Conclusion

Taken together, these reforms do not yet solve the backlog problem, nor do they eliminate the well-known structural challenges of judicial vacancies, inconsistent infrastructure, and resistance to procedural discipline. But they do suggest that the justice system is not static. Technology is being mainstreamed; specialised courts are being expanded; the very architecture of criminal law has been rebuilt; policy bodies are paying sustained attention; and alternative dispute-resolution is gaining statutory recognition. The pace may remain uneven, and implementation will require years of steady effort, but the direction is unmistakable.

Looking to the future, most experts agree that reforms must focus on a combination of better case management, deeper use of technology, a major increase in judge strength, and a more disciplined approach to adjournments. India will need stronger mediation systems, modern court administration, and more transparent judicial performance data. Courts must also shift towards a culture where judges actively manage timelines, evidence, and hearings rather than letting cases drift. Above all, reforms must address the root cause of much litigation: government departments continue to be the single largest litigants in the country. Reducing unnecessary government appeals could significantly reduce the overall burden on courts.

References

1. Law Commission of India. *Report No. 245: Arrears & Backlog — Creating Additional Judicial (Wo)man-power*. 2014. https://lawcommissionofindia.nic.in/report_twentieth/

2. Ministry of Law & Justice, Government of India. *E-Courts Mission Mode Project (Integrated Mission Mode Project for ICT enablement of the Indian Judiciary)*. December 2024. https://www.pib.gov.in/PressReleaseIframePage.aspx?PRID=2085127

3. Ministry of Law & Justice, Government of India. *The Mediation Act, 2023 (Act No 32 of 2023)*. 14 September 2023. https://legalaffairs.gov.in/sites/default/files/MediationAct2023.pdf

4. National Informatics Centre / eCommittee, Supreme Court of India. *eCourts Mission Mode Project: Policy & Action Plan Document Phase II*. 2013. Available at: https://ecourts.gov.in/ecourts_home/static/manuals/PolicyActionPlanDocument-PhaseII-approved-08012014-indexed_Sign.pdf

5. Ministry of Home Affairs. *Bharatiya Nyaya Sanhita (2023), Bharatiya Nagarik Suraksha Sanhita (2023), Bharatiya Sakshya Adhiniyam (2023).* Available at: https://www.mha.gov.in/sites/default/files/250883_english_01042024.pdf

6. NITI Aayog. *Annual Report 2024-25.* Available at: https://niti.gov.in/sites/default/files/2025-02/Annual%20Report%202024-25%20English_FINAL_LOW%20RES_0.pdf

Chapter 11: Conclusion

Delay in justice is more than an administrative inconvenience, it is a denial of a constitutional right. Article 21 of the Indian Constitution guarantees the right to personal liberty and fair procedure, and a system where cases linger for years inevitably violates that promise.

Across the chapters of this book, we have seen how delays arise from many sources: shortage of judges, slow investigations, complex laws, frequent adjournments, misuse of procedures, and lack of modern case management. Technology, including digital courts and AI-assisted tools, can help reduce the burden, but it cannot replace the need for more judges, better-trained staff, and a stronger administrative framework. The reforms introduced in recent years, from the Mediation Act to the large-scale digitisation of courts and the overhaul of criminal laws, show that change is possible, but much work remains.

However, technology and digitisation alone cannot solve pendency. Without sufficient judges, staff, and training, technology speeds up paperwork but not justice delivery.

All of this is no easy task. There has to be a concerted intention from both the government and the judiciary, to make the judicial system more user friendly, more just and to tackle the backlog. The reforms recommended by the various law commissions have to be implemented. All the suggested changes can take years or decades to be implemented, hence there has to be a sustained will to act.

The government and judiciary have to come together to seriously think and implement ways to tackle this problem. The people, on their part, have to keep up their activism and keep lobbying for judicial reforms that are necessary.

About the authors

Siva Prasad Bose is an electrical engineer and a writer of introductory guidebooks on different aspects of Indian laws. He is retired after many years of service in Uttar Pradesh Power Corporation Limited (formerly UPSEB). He received his engineering degree from Jadavpur University, Kolkata and law degree from Meerut University, Meerut. His interests lie in the fields of family law, civil law, law of contracts, and any areas of law related to power electricity related issues.

Joy Bose is a software engineer and data scientist with experience in machine learning and natural language processing. He has contributed to the writing and research of this book, with a particular focus on the role of technology and artificial intelligence in improving judicial efficiency. His interests include the application of data-driven tools to solve complex institutional problems, including the challenges facing India's legal system.

Glossary of Key Terms

Adjournment: The postponement of a court hearing to a later date. Repeated adjournments are one of the primary reasons for long delays in Indian courts.

Adverse Possession: A legal doctrine that allows a person who occupies another's land continuously and openly for a prescribed period (12 years in India) to claim ownership of it. This creates an incentive for illegal occupation of property.

Bail: The temporary release of an accused person awaiting trial, typically subject to conditions such as a monetary deposit or periodic reporting to the police. The difficulty of obtaining bail is a major cause of undertrial detention.

Bharatiya Nyaya Sanhita (BNS): The new Indian criminal code enacted in 2023, replacing the Indian Penal Code (IPC) of 1860. Part of a broader overhaul of criminal law that also included the Bharatiya Nagarik Suraksha Sanhita (replacing the Code of Criminal Procedure) and the Bharatiya Sakshya Adhiniyam (replacing the Evidence Act).

Cognizable Offence: A criminal offence for which a police officer may arrest the accused without a warrant.

Serious crimes such as murder, robbery, and rape are cognizable offences.

Civil Case: A legal dispute between two or more parties seeking compensation or other remedies rather than criminal punishment. Property disputes, divorce cases, and contract disputes are common civil cases.

Crore: A unit in the Indian numbering system equal to ten million (10,000,000). One crore rupees is equivalent to ten million rupees. Used in this book when referring to the scale of pending cases (e.g., "4.5 crore pending cases" means 45 million cases).

Disposal Rate: The ratio of cases decided by a court in a given period to the number of new cases filed in the same period. A disposal rate below 100% means the backlog is growing.

e-Courts: A government initiative to digitise court records and processes across India, enabling online case filing, status tracking, and virtual hearings. The project is implemented in multiple phases.

FIR (First Information Report): The document filed by the police when they receive information about a cognizable offence. The filing of an FIR marks the formal start of a criminal investigation. Police refusal to file FIRs is a significant problem discussed in this book.

IPC 498A: A provision of the Indian Penal Code (now Section 85 of the Bharatiya Nyaya Sanhita) that deals with cruelty by a husband or his relatives towards a wife, including dowry-related harassment. The section is non-bailable and has been the subject of debate regarding its misuse.

Lakh: A unit in the Indian numbering system equal to one hundred thousand (100,000). Used in this book when citing statistics (e.g., "6.4 lakh cases" means 640,000 cases).

Lok Adalat: Literally "people's court," a form of alternative dispute resolution established under the Legal Services Authorities Act, 1987. Awards made by Lok Adalats are deemed decrees of civil courts and are final and binding, with no appeal lying against them. They are widely used to settle motor accident claims, matrimonial disputes, and labour matters.

Mediation: A form of alternative dispute resolution in which a neutral third party (the mediator) helps disputing parties reach a mutually agreeable settlement. Unlike a judge, a mediator does not impose a decision. The Mediation Act of 2023 gave statutory recognition to this process in India.

National Judicial Data Grid (NJDG): An online database of orders, judgments, and case details of courts across India, maintained as part of the e-Courts project. It provides real-time data on pending cases and disposal rates at district and subordinate courts.

PIL (Public Interest Litigation): A legal action filed in a court of law for the enforcement of public interest or general interest. PILs can be filed by any citizen in the Supreme Court (Article 32) or High Court (Article 226) of India. While they have achieved significant social impact, they are also subject to misuse.

Pendency: The state of a case remaining undecided or awaiting a final verdict. High pendency refers to the accumulation of a large number of unresolved cases in a court.

Undertrial: A person who has been arrested and is in judicial custody (prison) while their trial is still ongoing and no verdict has been delivered. Because their guilt has not been established, undertrials are technically presumed innocent. India has a disproportionately high number of undertrials relative to its convicted prisoner population.

Other books by Siva Prasad Bose

Introduction to Wills and Probate

Senior Citizens Abuse in India

Introduction to negotiable instruments

Introduction to marriage laws in India

Neighbor Problems in India and what to do about them

Managing Court Cases with Mental Strength

Introduction to Patents and Patent Law in India

Introduction to Property Law in India

www.ingramcontent.com/pod-product-compliance
Lightning Source LLC
Chambersburg PA
CBHW070300220526
45465CB00004B/1674